I0049186

INVESTING

GROWING

WEALTH THROUGH

REAL ESTATE

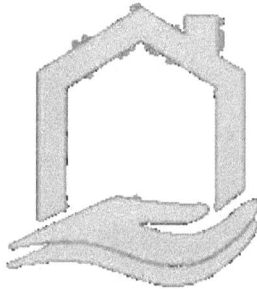

By

David S Phung, M.S.

Craig Cox, Contributor

Cindy Long, Contributor

Lisa Yu, Contributor

Precious McClain, Editor

Elizabeth B. Greer, Assistant Editor

David S. Phung, M.S., Author

Craig Cox, Contributor

Cindy Long, Contributor

Lisa Yu, Contributor

Precious McClain, Editor

Elizabeth B. Greer, Assistant Editor

David S. Phung, M.S., Author
Realtor DRE Lic: 01741202

Craig Cox, Contributor
California Real Estate Broker
Lic 01884300

Cindy Long, Contributor
Mortgage Loan Banker
NMLS #2083483

Lisa Yu, Contributor
Broker, Coldwell Banker
Realty CA DRE #01384900

Precious McClain, Editor
Over A Decade In Property Management
California Real Estate Lic
CCRM (California Certified Property Manager)

Elizabeth B. Greer, Assistant Editor
Realtor, Fusion Real Estate Network, Inc.

Author's Introduction

David S Phung's journey in real estate is more than just a career it's a calling. From the very start, he has approached the industry with dedication, an entrepreneurial spirit, and a genuine desire to help people make confident, life-changing decisions.

Based in Sacramento, California, David has become a trusted guide for both clients and colleagues. Known for his honesty, deep market knowledge, and ability to truly listen, he ensures that every client feels supported. For David, real estate isn't just about buying and selling property it's about building relationships and helping people achieve their dreams.

Today, he works with LPT Realty, Inc., though his career path has also taken him through some of the most respected names in the business, including Keller Williams Realty, eXp Realty, and Berkshire Hathaway HomeServices. With each role, his mission has remained the same: to help people navigate the complex world of real estate with clarity, confidence, and care.

David is also deeply engaged in the professional community, holding memberships with the Sacramento Association of Realtors, the California Association of Realtors, and the National Association of Realtors. In 2009, his efforts were recognized with a Certificate of Appreciation from the Realtor Action Fund Investor a testament to his dedication and belief in the importance of responsible homeownership.

While this book draws heavily on David's personal experience, knowledge, and passion, it is also the result of a team effort. His partners, teammates, and colleagues have played an important role in shaping the ideas, research, and strategies shared here. Their collaboration has strengthened the work, ensuring that it reflects a broader perspective and delivers even greater value to readers.

For David and his co-creators, success is not measured simply by the number of pages written, but by the lives positively impacted through the lessons and insights shared in this book.

Professional Experience

David's career has always been rooted in service and connection. Long before stepping into the world of real estate, he was learning the value of hard work and community impact. His professional journey began with the City of Sacramento's Central Services and the Summer Youth Employment Training Program, where he saw firsthand how dedication and teamwork could make a difference in people's lives.

In 1990, David took a leap of faith and followed his entrepreneurial instincts by starting his own business, Victor Printing. For nearly five years, he poured his heart into running the company, building relationships with customers, managing day-to-day operations, and finding creative ways to grow. That experience taught him lessons he still carries into his real estate work today: listen closely, follow through, and treat every client like they're your only one.

As his real estate career grew, so did his network. Over the years, David has worked side by side with loan officers, escrow and title experts, repair specialists, and inspection teams, learning the ins and outs of every step in the process. This hands-on experience has given him a 360-degree view of the industry and the ability to make transactions as smooth and stress-free as possible. Clients know they can count on him not just for results, but for guidance, patience, and genuine care every step of the way.

Education

David's academic achievements form the backbone of his professional excellence. He holds a Master of Science in Management Information Systems - Project Management from Golden Gate University - Sacramento Campus, San Francisco, CA. In addition, he earned dual Bachelor of Science degrees from California State University, Sacramento one in Business Administration (Strategic Management/Operations Management) and another in Graphic Design/Marketing.

He is also a proud graduate of the Sacramento Entrepreneurship Academy, where he earned a diploma in Entrepreneurship in 1997. David further expanded his expertise through participation in national leadership programs, including the U.S. Minority Business Development Agency's Emerging Business Leader Summit in Washington, D.C., and the U.S. Small Business Administration's 50-Year National Conference in Bay Lake, Florida.

A Message to Readers

This book is more than just strategies and tips; it's a blueprint for building lasting wealth, creating freedom, and taking control of your financial future.

Whether you're buying your first rental, flipping properties, or scaling a portfolio, the chapters ahead will guide you step-by-step through the tools, strategies, and mindset that have worked for me and countless others. My hope is that you'll finish this book not only with knowledge, but with the confidence to take action and the vision to see what's possible.

Your journey starts now. Let's build something great together.

To your success,

David S Phung

Disclaimer

The information presented in *Investing and Growing Wealth Through Real Estate* by David S Phung is provided for educational and informational purposes only. It should not be interpreted as financial, legal, tax, or investment advice. While every effort has been made to ensure the accuracy and reliability of the information in this book, the author and publisher make no guarantees regarding its completeness, accuracy, or suitability for your specific circumstances.

Real estate investing carries inherent risks, and outcomes will vary depending on individual situations, market conditions, and other factors beyond the author's control. Before acting on any strategies or concepts discussed in *Investing and Growing Wealth Through Real Estate*, you are strongly encouraged to seek guidance from qualified professionals, including licensed real estate agents, attorneys, accountants, and financial advisors, to determine what is right for your unique goals and needs.

Neither the author nor the publisher shall be held liable for any loss, damage, or other consequences that may arise, directly or indirectly, from the use or application of any information contained in this book. All decisions and actions are solely your responsibility.

Introduction

1. Story and Expertise

- Brief personal introduction and professional background in real estate.
- Why I wrote this book and how it can help readers achieve their real estate goals.

2. Who This Book is for

- First-time buyers, sellers, and those interested in profiting from real estate.
- Professionals and aspiring investors looking for practical advice and actionable guidance.

3. What Readers Will Learn

- Proven tips for profiting from real estate investments.
- Unique strategies and insights that set this book apart from others in the field.

Book Outline:

Part 3: Investing and Growing Wealth Through

Why Real Estate is a Powerful Investment

Overview of long-term wealth-building through real estate.

Types of Real Estate Investments

Rental properties, flipping houses, commercial real estate, etc.

Building Your Investment Strategy

Setting goals, understanding risks, and managing finances.

How to Identify Profitable Properties

Market research and analysis techniques.

Tools and resources to evaluate investment opportunities.

Owning and Managing Real Estate

Managing rental properties, tenants, and maintenance.

Legal and financial considerations for property ownership.

Scaling Your Real Estate Portfolio

How to grow your investments and achieve financial independence.

Financing Your First (and Next) Investment

Explore loan types: conventional, FHA/VA, DSCR, portfolio, and hard money.

Learn creative financing: seller carrybacks, subject-to deals, and lease options.

Navigating Taxes and Legal Structures

Use tax strategies like depreciation, 1031 exchanges, and cost segregation.

Choose the right legal entity (LLC, trust) for asset protection and liability control.

Understanding Market Cycles and Timing

Recognize cycle phases: recovery, expansion, hyper-supply, recession.

Adapt investment strategies to market trends and local economic indicators.

Risk Management and Due Diligence

Conduct thorough inspections, title checks, and market analysis.

Protect assets with insurance, reserves, and legal safeguards.

Partnering for Profits: Joint Ventures and Syndications

Structure joint ventures and partnerships for capital and skill-sharing.

Understand syndications (GPs and LPs) and how to vet investment partners.

Creative and Alternative Strategies

Explore lease options, wholesaling, and land or note investing.

Consider commercial properties for diversification and scale.

Conclusion

1. Recap of Key Points

   - Summarizing the buying, selling, and investing processes.

2. Next Steps for Readers

   - Encouraging readers to take action and apply the strategies.

3. Resources and Tools

   - List of helpful resources, websites, and contact information.

TABLE OF CONTENTS

Why Real Estate is Your Wealth-Building Superpower

Throughout history, empires, fortunes, and legacies have been built on one timeless asset: land. In the modern world, real estate remains a dominant and accessible vehicle for building wealth. Unlike volatile markets or abstract investments, real estate offers something tangible, resilient, and customizable. It is not merely a place to live or work; it is a tool that, when used wisely, has the power to transform financial futures. This chapter will unveil why real estate is not just an investment class but a genuine superpower for creating long-term wealth.

Leverage: Building Wealth with Other People's Money

One of the most powerful aspects of real estate is the ability to use leverage. When you purchase property with a mortgage, you are essentially controlling a large asset with a relatively small initial investment. This allows you to multiply your potential returns. Unlike stocks, where you pay full price per share, real estate lets you acquire a $300,000 asset with a 10-20% down payment, while the rest is financed by the bank. As the property appreciates and generates income, your returns grow exponentially relative to your initial outlay.

Cash Flow: Creating Monthly Passive Income

Real estate can provide a consistent and relatively predictable stream of passive income. Through rental properties, investors earn monthly income after expenses, commonly referred to as cash flow. This income stream can supplement or even replace employment income, offering freedom and financial security. When managed properly, real estate allows you to earn while you sleep.

Appreciation: Growing Your Wealth over Time

Over time, real estate tends to appreciate in value. While markets may fluctuate in the short term, the long-term trend historically shows that property values rise due to inflation, population growth, and demand for land. In addition to this natural appreciation, owners can increase a property's value through renovations, upgrades, and strategic repositioning a process known as forced appreciation.

Tax Advantages: Keeping More of What You Earn

Real estate offers unique tax benefits that most investments can't match. Through depreciation, owners can reduce taxable income on paper without spending money. Operating expenses, interest payments, and even travel related to property management can be deducted. Furthermore, tools like the 1031 exchange allow investors to defer capital gains taxes when selling and reinvesting in new properties, creating a powerful snowball effect.

Inflation Hedge: Protecting Your Wealth

Inflation erodes purchasing power over time, but real estate tends to move with inflation. As the cost of living increases, so do rents and property values. Owning real estate protects investors by keeping them on the profitable side of inflation, rather than being harmed by it. This built-in hedge is especially valuable in uncertain economic times.

Control: Shaping Your Investment

Unlike stocks or mutual funds, where you have no influence on performance, real estate gives you direct control over your investment. You can choose the property, improve it, manage tenants, adjust rents, or even refinance when the market is right. This level of control empowers you to directly impact the profitability and value of your asset.

Equity: Building Wealth with Every Payment

As tenants pay rent and you make mortgage payments, you build equity. Over time, the loan is paid down, and your ownership stake in the property increases. This combination of equity growth and property appreciation compounds your net worth significantly.

Legacy: Creating Generational Wealth

Real estate is an ideal vehicle for creating lasting wealth across generations. Properties can be passed down, providing income, shelter, or capital to future heirs. A well-structured real estate portfolio can serve as a financial fortress for your family, offering stability and opportunities that can span lifetimes.

Diversification: A Solid Addition to Your Portfolio

Adding real estate to your investment portfolio provides diversification, balancing risk from stocks, bonds, or other assets. Real estate often performs differently than the broader markets, offering a counterweight during economic downturns and helping protect your overall wealth.

Real-Life Success Stories

Consider a young couple who bought a duplex and rented out half while living in the other unit. Over a decade, they leveraged that one investment into several properties, built substantial equity, and eventually achieved financial independence. Their story and countless others like it demonstrate that real estate is not just a theoretical wealth-builder; it's a practical, proven path to lasting prosperity.

Conclusion

Real estate isn't just a good investment; it's a financial superpower. With the right knowledge, strategy, and discipline, it can unlock doors to freedom, abundance, and legacy. Whether you're just beginning your journey or looking to expand your portfolio, real estate offers unparalleled opportunities to build wealth on your terms.

Exploring Investment Options: From Rentals to Flipping

There is no one-size-fits-all path to real estate investing. The beauty of this field lies in its diversity. From steady, long-term rentals to quick-turnaround flips and everything in between, real estate offers numerous strategies tailored to different lifestyles, goals, and levels of risk tolerance. Whether you're looking for monthly income, long-term appreciation, or fast cash, there's an investment strategy for you. This chapter explores the most popular and effective real estate investment options, helping you find the right fit for your ambitions.

Long-Term Rentals: Steady Income and Lasting Growth

One of the most traditional and widely used real estate strategies is long-term renting. This involves buying residential properties such as single-family homes or apartment units and leasing them to tenants for extended periods. These investments generate consistent cash flow and benefit from both mortgage pay down and appreciation. Over time, long-term rentals can become stable, income-producing assets that offer excellent returns with manageable risks.

Short-Term Rentals: Maximizing Income with Flexibility

The rise of platforms like Airbnb and Vrbo has revolutionized the short-term rental market. Investors can rent properties by the night or week, often earning significantly more than they would from long-term leases. However, short-term rentals require more hands-on management, marketing, and attention to guest experience. They are also subject to local laws and regulations that may limit their use. For the right investor, this strategy offers high returns and creative freedom.

House Hacking: Live for Less While Building Equity

House hacking is a smart strategy for beginners. It involves purchasing a multi-unit property, living in one unit, and renting out the others. This allows the owner to offset or even eliminate housing costs while building equity and gaining landlord experience. It's also a powerful way to get started with minimal investment, especially when utilizing owner-occupied loan programs.

Fix and Flip: Turning Sweat Equity into Profit

Fix-and-flip investing involves purchasing distressed properties, renovating them, and selling them for a profit. This model relies heavily on accurate valuation, renovation expertise, and market timing. Flipping can be highly profitable but carries more risk than buy-and-hold strategies. Investors need a solid understanding of construction costs, timelines, and resale value to succeed.

The BRRRR Method: Build and Scale with Limited Capital

BRRRR (Buy, Rehab, Rent, Refinance, Repeat) is a strategy that allows investors to recycle capital and grow portfolios rapidly. After buying and renovating a property, the investor rents it out and then refinances based on the new value, recovering their initial investment. This capital can then be used to buy the next property. BRRRR is ideal for investors looking to scale without tying up too much cash.

Wholesaling: Making Money without Owning Property

Wholesaling is a strategy where investors find discounted properties, place them under contract, and then assign those contracts to other buyers for a fee. Wholesalers act as middlemen, earning profits by finding and negotiating deals. It's a great way to get into real estate with little to no capital, though it requires strong marketing, negotiation, and networking skills.

REITs: Real Estate Investing Without the Hassle

For those seeking a more passive approach, Real Estate Investment Trusts (REITs) offer exposure to real estate without the need to own or manage property. REITs are companies that own or finance income-producing real estate. Investors can buy shares much like stocks and receive dividends. This strategy is perfect for hands-off investors who want portfolio diversification and liquidity.

Commercial Real Estate: Higher Stakes, Higher Rewards

Investing in commercial real estate such as office buildings, retail centers, and warehouses offers the potential for significant income and appreciation. These properties often have longer leases and higher rental rates, but they also require more capital, expertise, and management. Commercial investing is not for everyone, but it can be a powerful wealth-building tool for seasoned investors.

Raw Land and Development: Building from the Ground Up

Land investing involves purchasing vacant lots or undeveloped land with the intent to hold, subdivide, or develop. Though it lacks immediate cash flow, land can appreciate significantly, especially in growing markets. Development projects can yield massive returns, but they require substantial planning, permits, capital, and risk management.

Creative Strategies: Thinking Outside the Traditional Box

Real estate also offers creative ways to finance and structure deals, such as seller financing, lease options, and subject-to agreements. These strategies can help investors acquire property with little money down or when traditional financing isn't available. Creativity often makes the difference between a good deal and a great one.

Finding Your Investment Path

Each investment strategy comes with its own benefits, challenges, and ideal investor profile. The key to success is choosing the path that aligns with your financial goals, available time, risk tolerance, and personal interests. Some investors thrive on the thrill of flipping, while others prefer the stability of long-term rentals. The best strategy is the one you can commit to, learn deeply, and execute consistently.

Conclusion

Real estate investing is not a one-road journey; it's an entire map of opportunities. Whether you want cash flow, appreciation, flexibility, or scalability, there's a strategy tailored to you. Understanding your options is the first step toward building a profitable, rewarding real estate business. The next step? Taking action on the one that calls to you most.

The Smart Investor's Toolkit –
Evaluating Properties for Profit

Every successful real estate investor has one thing in common: the ability to analyze deals with clarity, confidence, and accuracy. Emotions may influence first impressions, but numbers and strategy are what drive long-term success. The smartest investors approach each opportunity with discipline. They rely on measurable indicators, in-depth research, and well-honed instincts developed over time. This chapter will give you a complete toolkit to evaluate potential real estate investments from a profit-first perspective. You will learn how to define your strategy, understand key financial metrics, analyze market dynamics, and build data-backed preforms that illuminate the true potential of any property you consider.

Defining Your Investment Strategy

Before you start crunching numbers, you must clearly define what success looks like for you. Some investors pursue cash flow that provides monthly passive income, while others focus on long-term appreciation in growing markets. There are those who prefer short-term flips for fast profits, and others who find security in stable rental income. Your strategy whether it's buy-and-hold, fix-and-flip, or BRRRR (buy, rehab, rent, refinance, repeat) must align with your personal goals, risk tolerance, and available resources. This clarity will serve as a compass for evaluating every deal that crosses your desk.

Core Financial Metrics That Drive Decision-Making

Real estate investing is a numbers game. To identify a profitable opportunity, you must understand and apply the right financial metrics. Cash flow is the lifeblood of any rental investment. It represents the income left after all expenses are paid. The capitalization rate, or cap rate, provides a quick estimate of return based on net operating income and purchase price. Return on investment (ROI) allows you to measure how efficiently your money is working, while the internal rate of return (IRR) accounts for the value of money over time. Another crucial metric is the debt service coverage ratio (DSCR), which shows whether the property generates enough income to cover loan payments. Each of these numbers tells a different part of the story. When used together, they give a well-rounded view of a property's performance.

Valuation Methods and Their Applications

Determining a property's true value requires more than a quick glance at listing prices. Professional investors and appraisers use three primary valuation methods: the sales comparison approach, the cost approach, and the income approach. The sales comparison method looks at recent sales of similar properties to estimate value. It is particularly useful for residential homes. The cost approach estimates what it would cost to rebuild the property from scratch, adjusted for depreciation often applied to new construction. The income approach, favored for income-producing assets, values the property based on how much revenue it generates. Knowing which method to use and when will guide your buying decisions and negotiating strategy.

Evaluating Market and Neighborhood Fundamentals

Even a great property can underperform in the wrong location. This is why market research is just as critical as property analysis. Start by studying broader market conditions such as job growth, population trends, and rental demand. Then narrow your focus to the neighborhood level. Look for indicators of growth like new infrastructure projects, commercial development, and gentrification. Proximity to schools, transportation, and amenities adds value, while high crime rates or poor municipal services are warning signs. The goal is to invest in areas with strong fundamentals that support appreciation and tenant demand.

Conducting a Full Pro Forma Analysis

A pro forma is a forward-looking financial statement that estimates how a property will perform over time. It includes projected rental income, vacancy rates, operating expenses, and loan costs. Building a proforma forces you to examine every income stream and expense category, from property taxes and insurance to utilities and maintenance. Once completed, it reveals your net operating income, debt service obligations, and projected cash flow. The pro forma also allows you to run "what-if" scenarios, testing the impact of rent increases, expense hikes, or extended vacancies. This is where an investor transforms raw numbers into strategic insights.

Using Technology to Your Advantage

In the digital age, investors no longer need to rely solely on spreadsheets and gut feelings. Powerful tools are available to analyze properties, compare deals, and research neighborhoods in minutes. Online platforms can automate calculations, generate preforms, and even provide real-time market data. By integrating these technologies into your process, you not only save time but also gain a competitive edge. The best investors today are both analytical and tech-savvy, leveraging every available tool to sharpen their decision-making and scale their portfolios efficiently.

Go or No-Go: Making the Final Investment Call

Once you've done your due diligence, it's time to decide whether to move forward. This is where analysis meets instinct. Review the numbers, reflect on your goals, and assess your comfort with the risks involved. No deal is perfect, but the right deal should align with your strategy, offer acceptable returns, and fall within your capacity to manage. This final decision should be based on facts, not pressure or emotion. A disciplined investor knows when to walk away and when to commit with confidence.

Before signing on the dotted line, always schedule a final walkthrough typically done three to five days before closing. This step ensures that the property is in the agreed-upon condition, that any negotiated repairs have been completed, and that no new issues have appeared since your inspection. It is your last opportunity to confirm the property meets expectations before ownership transfers. Skipping this step can leave you with unpleasant and costly surprises, but handling it diligently protects both your investment and your peace of mind.

Owning and Managing Properties like a Pro

Buying a property is only the first step. What follows is the real test of your ability to turn an asset into a sustainable, income-generating business. Property management is where profit margins are made or lost. Whether you choose to manage properties yourself or hire a professional manager, you must understand the principles of ownership, operations, maintenance, and tenant relations. This chapter shows you how to manage real estate like a business: with structure, systems, and strategy. You'll learn how to build a profitable operation, avoid legal trouble, and create a solid foundation for long-term portfolio growth.

Choosing the Best Ownership Structure

The structure you choose for holding your properties affects everything from taxes to liability. Sole ownership may work for beginners, but it offers little protection. Partnerships allow you to combine resources but require careful planning and legal agreements. Many investors form limited liability companies (LLCs) to separate their personal assets from business liabilities. Others use trusts or corporations for estate planning or tax advantages. The right choice depends on your long-term goals, risk tolerance, and legal advice. Establishing a solid foundation here will save you from complications later.

Navigating Financing and Refinancing Options

Property ownership is a dynamic process. Your financing strategy must evolve along with your portfolio. Refinancing can help you lower monthly payments, access equity for reinvestment, or restructure debt for better terms. Investors also use tools like home equity lines of credit, cross-collateralization, and portfolio loans to manage capital and scale effectively. Understanding when and how to refinance allows you to optimize your cash flow and build long-term wealth through smart use of leverage.

Establishing a Property Management System

Property management is about systems and consistency. Whether you self-manage or outsource, there must be processes for tenant screening, rent collection, maintenance coordination, and lease enforcement. Technology can help automate many of these functions, but ultimately, success depends on clear communication, documented procedures, and responsiveness. A good system reduces stress, increases tenant satisfaction, and protects your bottom line.

What's included in a Property Management Fee?

If you decide to hire a property manager, understanding their fee structure is critical. Most property managers charge a percentage of monthly rent, but investors often overlook what that fee actually includes. Typical services may cover photography for listings, marketing campaigns, showing the property, screening tenants, handling negotiations, and preparing lease paperwork. Many also provide essentials like property signage and flyers to attract prospective renters.

Beyond placement, full-service managers handle ongoing rent collection, tenant communication, routine inspections, and maintenance coordination. However, not all services are automatically included in the standard fee. Some managers may charge extra for things like eviction filings, large renovation oversight, or specialized advertising. As an owner, always request a clear breakdown so you know exactly what's covered and what could lead to additional costs.

Tenant Relations: Screening, Retention, and Legalities

Your relationship with tenants directly impacts your profitability. The first step is thorough, legal screening checking credit, income, and references. Once tenants are in place, proactive communication, timely repairs, and respectful service go a long way toward retention. A well-drafted lease sets expectations and provides legal protection, but it must be enforced consistently. Understanding fair housing laws and staying compliant ensures you operate ethically and avoid legal pitfalls.

Maintenance, Repairs, and Capital Projects

Deferred maintenance is one of the quickest ways to erode property value and tenant trust. Preventative upkeep should be planned and budgeted as part of your annual operations. Set aside reserves for unexpected repairs and schedule regular inspections to catch small issues before they grow. Over time, you may also consider capital improvements like new roofs, wood-destroying pest control, upgraded appliances, or energy-efficient systems that enhance property value and attract better tenants. Effective maintenance protects your investment and reduces turnover.

Bookkeeping, Cash Flow, and Tax Optimization

Owning property is a business, and every business needs accurate books. Track all income and expenses, categorize them properly, and keep receipts and documentation. Use software to streamline bookkeeping and generate reports. Understanding cash flow patterns helps you plan for repairs, evaluate performance, and prepare for tax season. Real estate offers powerful tax advantages, including depreciation, mortgage interest deductions, and capital gains treatment. A good accountant is your partner in maximizing these benefits while staying compliant with regulations.

Legal Compliance and Risk Management

As a landlord, you operate in a highly regulated environment. Complying with local, state, and federal laws is essential. This includes fair housing regulations, landlord-tenant laws, safety codes, and eviction procedures. Insurance is another critical aspect of risk management. Property insurance, liability coverage, and umbrella policies can protect you from lawsuits and disasters. Keeping updated leases, documenting all interactions, and having legal counsel available helps you avoid costly legal battles.

Scaling Your Portfolio

Once your systems are in place, the next step is growth. Scaling requires planning. Analyze your current properties to identify what's working and what can be improved. As you add more units, your time becomes more valuable, and delegation becomes necessary. Consider building a team of professional's property managers, contractors, lenders, and advisors who support your goals. Growth should be strategic and sustainable, allowing you to replicate success without burning out.

Exit Strategies and Generational Wealth

Every investment eventually comes full circle. Whether you plan to sell, refinance, or pass your properties to the next generation, you need an exit strategy. Selling outright may yield immediate profits, while a 1031 exchange allows you to defer capital gains taxes by reinvesting in a similar property. For long-term legacy planning, trusts and estate plans ensure your assets are preserved and transferred according to your wishes. Real estate isn't just about income it's about creating wealth that lasts.

Scaling Up: Building a Real Estate Portfolio for Long-Term Growth

R eaching the stage of portfolio expansion is a milestone that marks the transition from being a beginner investor to becoming a strategic wealth builder. Scaling up in real estate is not simply about acquiring more properties it's about building a system, leveraging resources efficiently, and laying the foundation for long-term generational wealth. This chapter will equip you with the mindset, financial strategies, team-building insights, and operational systems you need to scale your portfolio sustainably and successfully.

The Mindset Shift: From Investor to Portfolio Builder

Before scaling, an investor must adopt a different way of thinking. Owning one or two properties may require a simple operational focus, but scaling to ten or twenty units and beyond requires strategic leadership. You must view your real estate journey as a business, with processes, people, and systems working together. Long-term thinking becomes essential, and patience is paramount. Every decision should align with your broader investment vision, whether that is financial independence, early retirement, or legacy creation.

Portfolio Growth Strategies

There are several pathways to grow your portfolio, and selecting the right one depends on your financial position, experience level, and market conditions. One common strategy is the BRRRR method Buy, Rehab, Rent, Refinance and Repeat, which allows investors to recycle capital while increasing property value. Alternatively, investors can grow through 1031 exchanges, which defer capital gains taxes when selling one investment property and purchasing another. Strategic scaling can also involve acquiring value-add properties, repositioning underperforming assets, or investing across different markets to reduce geographic risk.

Creative and Scalable Financing Options

As you scale, financing challenges evolve. While traditional mortgages may work for your first few properties, banks eventually impose lending limits. To overcome this, many investors transition to portfolio loans, blanket loans, or private funding solutions. Scaling also becomes more efficient through equity harvesting using the value appreciation of existing properties to fund new acquisitions via cash-out refinancing or home equity lines of credit (HELOCs). Understanding how to optimize debt and equity is a critical skill for the serious portfolio builder.

Building a High-Performance Real Estate Team

No successful investor scales alone. To manage a growing portfolio, you'll need to assemble a team of trusted professionals. Property managers can handle tenant relations and day-to-day operations, freeing you to focus on acquisition and strategy. You'll also need a real estate-savvy CPA to help optimize your tax strategy, an attorney for legal structuring and asset protection, and reliable contractors for renovations and repairs. This team becomes the backbone of your business, enabling efficient operations and faster decision-making.

Systems and Automation for Scalability

As the number of properties increases, manual processes become unsustainable. To maintain quality and efficiency, successful investors implement systems and technology. Property management software streamlines rent collection, maintenance tracking, and tenant communication. Automated accounting systems help manage income and expenses across multiple units. From leasing templates to customer relationship management (CRM) tools, automation is the secret to reducing time consumption and human error while maintaining control over your expanding operation.

Risk Management and Legal Structuring

With more properties comes more exposure to risk. Portfolio investors must proactively mitigate risk through insurance, diversification, and proper legal structuring. Adequate coverage should include liability protection, rent loss, and natural disaster insurance. Diversifying across different cities or property types can help insulate your portfolio from localized downturns. Legal structures such as LLCs or holding companies can provide protection against lawsuits and simplify tax filings. Advanced investors may also explore the use of series LLCs or family trusts for asset protection and estate planning.

Tracking Performance across the Portfolio

A large portfolio is only as strong as its performance. Investors must track key metrics such as total return on investment, debt service coverage ratio, net operating income, and occupancy rates. These figures inform whether properties should be held, improved, or sold. Strategic portfolio reviews ideally done quarterly help identify opportunities for refinancing, rent increases, or capital improvements. Consistent performance monitoring ensures that your entire portfolio continues to support your financial goals.

Planning for Exit and Legacy

At some point, every investor must decide how they want to exit or pass on their portfolio. Some may choose to liquidate assets for a lump-sum retirement fund, while others may prefer to transition properties into trusts for their children. Early planning enables tax efficiency and ensures a smoother transfer of wealth. Exit strategies should be built into the portfolio plan from the beginning and revisited as the portfolio matures and your life circumstances evolve.

Financing Your First (and Next) Investment

L et's be real buying your first investment property is exciting… and nerve-wracking. There's a good chance you're wondering, "How in the world am I supposed to afford this?" That's where financing comes in, and it's arguably one of the most powerful tools in real estate investing. When used right, financing doesn't just help you buy one property it helps you build a portfolio and grow real, lasting wealth.

This chapter isn't just about mortgages and paperwork. It's about learning how to use money yours and other people's to build something bigger than you could with cash alone.

The Power of Leverage (and Why It Matters So Much)

If you've ever heard the term "leverage" in real estate, here's what it means in plain terms: you're using borrowed money to buy an asset that's worth a lot more than what you're putting down. Say you buy a $300,000 rental with $60,000 of your own money and borrow the rest. That $60K gives you control of the full $300K asset and all of the rental income and potential appreciation that comes with it.

That's the magic of leverage. It lets your money work harder than it could in a savings account or even the stock market.

But like any tool, leverage has its risks. If your property sits empty, or if the market dips, that debt still needs to be paid. So, the goal is to be smart, not reckless. Treat debt with respect, and it'll work in your favor.

Getting Your First Loan: Where Most People Start

For your first property, most people go the traditional route a standard mortgage from a bank. These are often backed by big government entities like Fannie Mae or Freddie Mac. They're relatively safe, offer good interest rates, and have predictable terms. You'll typically need a down payment of 15–25%, a decent credit score, and a stable income.

But there are special programs that can make it easier to get in the game. FHA loans, for example, let you put down as little as 3.5%. The catch? You need to live in the property for at least a year. This is why many first-time investors start with "house hacking" buying a duplex or triplex, living in one unit, and renting out the others. It's a clever way to ease into investing while building equity.

If you're a veteran, VA loans are a hidden gem. No down payment, no private mortgage insurance, and solid terms. It's one of the best tools out there if you qualify.

Now, if your credit or income doesn't quite fit the mold, don't panic. Portfolio lenders usually smaller, local banks might still work with you. These lenders keep the loans in-house instead of selling them, so they're often more flexible, especially for unique properties or self-employed borrowers.

And then there are hard money and private loans. These aren't for everyone, but they move fast and focus more on the value of the deal than your financial history. They're great for flips or short-term plays but come with higher interest rates and tighter timelines.

Before You Apply: What You Need to Have Ready

Before you walk into a lender's office (or even apply online), there are a few things you need to get in order.

First up: your credit. Aim for at least a 680 score, but higher is better. Pull your report, fix any errors, pay down high balances, and avoid taking on new debt right before applying. Your credit score directly affects your interest rate and loan terms, so it pays literally to get it right.

Beyond your score, lenders also want to see a track record. A good rule of thumb is to have at least three active trade lines reporting on your credit report. These could be credit cards, auto loans, student loans, or other credit accounts. Having three or more trade lines shows lenders you can responsibly manage different types of debt over time.

And here's a mistake to avoid: opening new credit cards right before applying for a mortgage. Even if the offers look tempting, new accounts and inquiries can temporarily lower your score and raise red flags for lenders. Stick with your existing accounts, keep them in good standing, and show a consistent payment history.

It also helps to choose an experienced loan officer who understands investment properties, not just standard home mortgages. The right loan officer can guide you through the process, anticipate challenges, and structure your application in the best light for approval.

Next, lenders want to see stable income usually two years' worth. If you're a W2 employee, that's easy. If you're self-employed or a freelancer, you'll need tax returns and good bookkeeping to prove your earnings.

They'll also look at your debt-to-income ratio, or DTI. That's the percentage of your income that's already going toward other debts (car payments, student loans, credit cards, etc.). Lower is better ideally under 43%.

And finally, you'll need cash. Not just for the down payment, but also for closing costs, reserves, and unexpected expenses. Many investors save aggressively, but others tap into creative sources home equity lines, 401(k) loans, or even gifts from family. However you do it, make sure your funds are documented and ready to go.

So, You Bought One Property what's next?

Once your first rental is up and running, it's time to think bigger. This is where scaling becomes more about strategy than saving.

One of the best strategies for growing a portfolio is the BRRRR method Buy, Rehab, Rent, Refinance and Repeat. You buy a fixer-upper, renovate it to boost the value, rent it out, and then refinance to pull your money back out. With that cash, you can go buy another property and do it again.

Another common method is a cash-out refinance. If your property has gone up in value or you've paid down the mortgage, you can refinance and take out the difference as cash. That's capital you can use for your next deal without selling the original property.

You can also tap into a HELOC (Home Equity Line of Credit), which works like a revolving credit line secured by your equity. It's a flexible way to fund down payments or renovations.

If you're hitting a wall with traditional lenders, consider seller financing. In this setup, the seller acts like the bank you agree on terms, interest, and monthly payments. It's especially useful when the property doesn't qualify for a mortgage or the seller is motivated and willing to negotiate.

And don't underestimate the power of partnerships. You might find someone with capital but no time, while you have time and deal-making skills. If structured right, partnerships can accelerate your growth just be clear on roles, responsibilities, and profit splits.

Creative Financing for the Bold and Strategic

Once you're comfortable in the game, you might start exploring more creative options. "Subject-to" financing, for example, involves taking over the seller's existing mortgage payments without formally assuming the loan. It's a way to acquire property with little to no money down, but it does come with legal and ethical complexities, so get expert advice.

Lease options also known as rent-to-own let you control a property and earn income while delaying the purchase. This can be a great stepping stone if you're light on cash or credit.

For larger, more complex deals, syndications come into play. You can pool money with other investors to buy multifamily buildings, commercial properties, or development projects. Typically, there's a lead investor (the general partner) who handles operations, while others contribute money as limited partners. It's more advanced, but it's how many seasoned investors grow into serious wealth.

The People Who Help Make It Happen

Your financing journey gets a whole lot easier when you've got the right people in your corner. Build relationships with lenders who understand real estate investing. Local banks and credit unions are often more flexible than big national banks, and they tend to treat you like a person, not just an application.

Beyond lenders, surround yourself with a good mortgage broker, a real estate-savvy CPA, a solid attorney, and a trustworthy title company. These people are your financial team, and they'll help you structure deals, avoid pitfalls, and build wealth smartly.

How Lenders Look at You and Your Deal

Lenders aren't just handing out money they're assessing risk. They want to know that your deal makes sense. That means looking at your loan-to-value (LTV) ratio, which tells them how much equity you have in the deal. They also care about your debt service coverage ratio (DSCR), which compares the property's net income to the loan payments. If your DSCR is above 1.2, that's a good sign the property can cover itself.

They'll also want to see cash flow projections, a plan for managing the property, and that you have reserves in case something goes wrong. A well-organized loan package makes you look professional and trustworthy.

Common Mistakes to Avoid

It's easy to get excited and move too fast, but overleveraging can quickly become a nightmare. Too much debt and not enough cash flow can turn a promising investment into a stress machine. Adjustable-rate loans can also be risky if you're not prepared for rising payments.

Another common mistake? Banking on appreciation. Yes, property values often go up, but that's not guaranteed. Your deal should work based on cash flow first, not future hope.

And don't forget about reserves. You'll need money for vacancies, repairs, and surprises. A single bad month shouldn't derail your entire investment plan.

Matching Financing to Your Strategy

Different types of investments call for different types of financing. Buy-and-hold rentals work best with stable, long-term mortgages. Flips need fast funding, like hard money or private loans. The BRRRR method blends both. House hackers can start with FHA or VA loans, while short-term rental investors might need special loans that account for seasonal income.

There's no one-size-fits-all. The best loan for the job depends on your goals, your strategy, and your experience level.

Final Thoughts: Financing is the Foundation

At the end of the day, financing isn't just a hurdle it's your superpower.

Navigating Taxes and Legal Structures

Taxes and Legal Structures

Two areas that many real estate investors tend to ignore or postpone can be the difference between growing real wealth or losing chunks of it to the government or legal missteps. While they may not be as thrilling as negotiating a deal or remodeling a kitchen, they're critical pieces of the puzzle. This chapter is about understanding how to protect your assets, minimize taxes legally, and structure your investments to scale safely and efficiently.

Think of this part of your real estate journey as building the foundation under your financial house. Without it, everything you build could be at risk.

Why Taxes and Legal Structures Matter

It's easy to get caught up in cash flow, appreciation, and deal-making. But taxes can quietly erode your profits if you're not proactive. Real estate comes with unique tax advantages depreciation, 1031 exchanges, capital gains treatment but you have to know how to use them.

On the legal side, structuring your business properly protects you from lawsuits, limits liability, and helps you scale with less risk. You're not just an investor now you're a business owner. And business owners think in terms of asset protection, entity selection, and long-term planning.

Tax Basics Every Real Estate Investor Should Understand

Let's start with the basics. The money you earn from real estate generally falls into a few categories:

1. **Rental income** – This is the monthly rent you collect from tenants.

2. **Capital gains** – This is profit you make from selling a property.

3. **Depreciation and deductions** – These are paper losses you can use to lower your taxable income.

4. Rental income is taxed as ordinary income, but you can reduce your tax burden with operating expenses. Everything from mortgage interest to property management fees, repairs, and even travel to the property can be deducted if it's part of your investment business.

5. Depreciation is one of real estate's most powerful tax advantages. The IRS lets you "depreciate" the structure (not the land) over 27.5 years for residential properties. This non-cash deduction can often offset much or all of your rental income, leaving you with cash flow in your pocket but little to no tax owed on it.

6. When you sell a property, if you've owned it more than a year, any profit is considered a long-term capital gain, which is

usually taxed at a lower rate than your regular income. And if you want to defer those taxes altogether, you can do a 1031 exchange a strategy that allows you to roll your profits into a new property and defer capital gains tax indefinitely.

7. But remember: the IRS will want its cut eventually especially when depreciation is "recaptured" during a sale, unless you use strategies like 1031 exchanges or estate planning to offset it.

Entity Structures: Should You Use an LLC or Stay in Your Name?

One of the biggest questions new investors ask is whether they should buy property in their own name or set up a legal entity like an LLC (Limited Liability Company). The answer depends on your goals, risk tolerance, and plans for growth.

Owning property in your personal name is simple and works fine for your first rental or a house hack. It's easy to finance, requires no special setup, and keeps things uncomplicated. However, if something goes wrong a tenant sues you or someone is injured on the property your personal assets could be at risk.

That's where an LLC comes in. LLCs separate your personal assets from your business. If you're sued, only the assets in the LLC are exposed, not your home, car, or bank accounts. This creates a legal barrier between your investment activity and your personal life.

Setting up an LLC is straightforward in most states. You file with your state, pay a small fee, and get an EIN (Employer Identification

Number). You'll also need a business bank account and must keep your business finances separate from your personal ones.

LLCs also offer pass-through taxation, meaning the income flows through to your personal tax return (unless you elect otherwise), but without double taxation like a corporation.

But here's the catch: financing can get trickier. Most lenders won't give a conventional mortgage to an LLC unless it's a commercial loan. So, many investors buy properties in their name first, then transfer them into an LLC via a quitclaim deed or land trust though this can sometimes trigger the lender's "due on sale" clause. It's best to consult an attorney or real estate CPA before moving properties into an LLC.

For larger portfolios, some investors create a holding company structure one parent LLC owns other LLCs, each holding a different property or group of properties. This can offer stronger asset protection and organization, but it's more complex and requires solid bookkeeping.

S Corporations, C Corporations, and Trusts: When and Why to Use Them

Beyond LLCs, there are other entities to consider but only when you're at the stage where they make sense.

An **S Corporation** is often used for real estate-related businesses, such as property management or flipping, but not typically for rental properties. That's because S Corps don't allow for depreciation losses in the same way as LLCs. However, they do help reduce self-employment tax when you're earning active income, like commissions or fees.

C Corporations, on the other hand, offer more separation and permanence but come with double taxation unless structured carefully. Most small and mid-size investors don't need a C Corp unless they're running a high-revenue real estate business that needs retained earnings.

Trusts are more about estate planning and long-term asset protection. A revocable living trust helps you pass real estate to heirs without probate. An irrevocable trust offers stronger asset protection but removes your control of the asset. Some investors use land trusts to hold title to properties anonymously, often in combination with an LLC.

Bookkeeping and Tax Preparation: Treat It like a Business

If you want to grow your real estate portfolio beyond a couple of rentals, you must treat your investing like a business. That means professional bookkeeping, clean records, and a proactive tax strategy.

Keep personal and business finances separate. Open a dedicated business checking account. Use software like QuickBooks, Stessa, or Buildium to track income and expenses. Keep receipts, mileage logs, contractor invoices, and repair documentation.

Come tax season, don't rely on a basic tax preparer. You need a real estate-savvy CPA someone who understands depreciation schedules, cost segregation studies, passive loss rules, and 1031 exchanges. A good CPA won't just file your return they'll help you strategize to legally lower your tax bill.

Strategies for Reducing Taxes (Legally)

Here are a few tax strategies every investor should be aware of:

- **Cost Segregation:** Instead of depreciating everything over 27.5 years, this engineering-based study breaks out certain components (like appliances, fixtures, and carpet) that can be depreciated faster, increasing your paper losses early on.

- **Bonus Depreciation:** This allows you to deduct a large portion of certain property costs in the first year. The rules are phasing out over time, but they're still incredibly valuable while available.

- **1031 Exchange:** As mentioned earlier, this lets you defer capital gains taxes when you sell one investment property and roll the profits into another "like-kind" property. There are strict timelines and rules, so it must be done carefully.

- **Real Estate Professional Status:** If you or your spouse qualify, you can use real estate losses to offset active income. This can be a game-changer for high-income households investing in real estate.

- **Qualified Business Income (QBI) Deduction:** In some cases, rental real estate qualifies as a trade or business, giving you access to a 20% deduction on pass-through income.

- These strategies aren't loopholes they're part of the tax code. But you must know how to apply them correctly, and that's where expert advice becomes invaluable.

Protecting Your Assets: Insurance and Liability Considerations

Legal structures aren't your only defense against risk. You also need the right insurance coverage. Every property should have landlord insurance (not just standard homeowners insurance), which covers loss of rent, liability, and damage caused by tenants or disasters.

You should also consider umbrella insurance, which provides extra liability protection beyond your landlord policy often for just a few hundred dollars a year. This is a smart, affordable way to protect your growing net worth.

If you run a short-term rental, you'll need specialized insurance, as traditional landlord policies often don't cover guests or business use.

Final Thoughts: Build to Last, Not Just to Grow

If you plan to invest in more than one or two properties, structuring your business and tax strategy from the start isn't optional it's essential. You wouldn't build a high-rise on sand, and you shouldn't build your real estate portfolio on a shaky legal or tax foundation either.

The good news? You don't have to become a tax attorney or CPA. But you do need to understand enough to ask smart questions, hire the right professionals, and make decisions that align with your goals.

Real estate offers one of the most tax-advantaged, wealth-building paths available but only if you're proactive about protecting what you build.

Understanding Market Cycles and Timing

In real estate, timing isn't everything, but it's close. A great property bought at the wrong time can become a headache, while a good deal timed well can become the foundation of a fortune. The market doesn't move in a straight line, and if you want to build sustainable wealth, you need to understand how real estate cycles work and how to use them to your advantage.

Most investors learn about timing the hard way. This chapter helps you avoid that by learning how to recognize shifts, anticipate downturns, and position yourself for opportunity not panic when the market moves.

What Is a Real Estate Market Cycle?

Real estate, like the broader economy, moves in cycles. These cycles repeat over time, though not always in a predictable pattern or fixed timeline. Understanding where we are in the cycle can help you make smarter investment decisions whether that means buying aggressively, holding steady, or selling and sitting on cash.

Generally, the real estate market moves through four main phases:

1. **Recovery**

2. **Expansion**

3. **Hyper Supply**

4. **Recession**

Each phase affects prices, rents, demand, and competition in different ways. Let's walk through them one by one.

Phase 1: Recovery – The Silent Opportunity

This is the phase right after a downturn. The economy is sluggish, vacancies are high, and property values are low. Most people are still hesitant to buy or invest bad memories of the last crash linger. But beneath the surface, things are beginning to improve. Employment is stabilizing, interest rates may be low, and early investors are quietly entering the market.

This is often the best time to buy. Prices are depressed, competition is low, and sellers are more negotiable. If you can spot the signs of recovery early rising rents, slow but steady job growth, increased property inquiries you can get in ahead of the crowd.

The challenge? It doesn't feel good to buy during recovery. Fear dominates the headlines, and cash is tight. But this is where long-term wealth is born by moving in when others are still cautious.

Phase 2: Expansion – Growth and Confidence Return

Now the economy is heating up. Jobs are being created, consumer confidence is rising, and demand for housing increases. Vacancies are falling, rents are climbing, and new construction begins to pick up.

This phase can last several years. It's when most investors get active and when it feels "safe" to buy. Financing becomes easier to obtain, home values rise, and appreciation accelerates. As competition increases, it gets harder to find "deals," but there's still money to be made, especially through strategic upgrades, development, or adding value.

This is the time to grow your portfolio smartly. Don't overpay or stretch yourself too thin. Know your numbers, and avoid getting caught up in bidding wars or overestimating future appreciation. Expansion is profitable, but not without risk if you get swept up in the optimism.

Phase 3: Hyper Supply – Warning Signs Flashing

At some point, supply begins to outpace demand. Developers have been building aggressively, inventory rises, and vacancies begin to creep up. Rents plateau or even drop. Prices may still climb briefly due to inertia, but cracks are forming.

This is the phase where seasoned investors start to get cautious. The smart money begins to pull back, sell off weaker assets, or refinance while interest rates are still favorable. Less experienced investors may keep buying, thinking the boom will never end.

Timing here is crucial. If you're holding properties, it's time to ensure your cash flow is solid and your portfolio is stable. If you're flipping or speculating, now is the time to either exit or proceed very carefully. You can still make money in hyper supply, but only if you're nimble and aware of the risks.

Phase 4: Recession – Correction and Reset

Eventually, the bubble bursts or the economy cools. This may be triggered by rising interest rates, job losses, inflation, or external shocks. Prices fall, foreclosures rise, and demand dries up. Negative headlines dominate the news. Financing tightens up, and many overleveraged investors are forced to sell.

This is a painful phase but also an incredible opportunity for prepared investors. If you've kept your cash reserves strong and haven't overleveraged, you can start buying at significant discounts.

During a recession, the goal is survival first, then opportunity. Focus on managing your existing properties, keeping vacancies low, reducing expenses, and staying liquid. And when the dust settles? That's your moment. The next recovery phase is just around the corner.

How to Identify Where the Market Is

No cycle looks exactly the same, and timing the market perfectly is nearly impossible. But there are signs you can watch for:

- **Interest rates**: Rising rates usually signal we're moving toward hyper supply or recession. Falling rates can signal recovery or early expansion.

- **Vacancy rates**: Higher vacancies can mean hyper supply or recession. Falling vacancies usually point to recovery or expansion.

- **New construction permits**: A surge in permits often precedes a move into hyper supply.

- **Days on market (DOM)**: When listings sit longer, buyer demand is weakening.

- **Rent growth trends**: Slowing rent growth can indicate supply is catching up with demand.

- **Employment data**: Job growth fuels demand. Rising unemployment is a red flag.

- **Consumer sentiment**: Optimism usually peaks during hyper supply and crashes in recession.

It's not about guessing the future perfectly. It's about paying attention and adjusting your strategy based on what's actually happening.

National vs. Local Cycles: Not All Markets Move Together

One critical thing to understand: real estate is local. While the national economy plays a role, individual markets can be in very different phases at the same time.

For example, a fast-growing tech city like Austin might be in expansion while a midwestern industrial town is still in recovery. Coastal markets may overheat and correct faster, while smaller secondary cities may remain more stable.

As an investor, always study your local market fundamentals population growth, job trends, infrastructure investment, housing supply, rental demand before making decisions.

This is especially important if you're investing out of state or remotely. Don't assume what's happening nationally applies to your chosen market.

Strategies Based on the Cycle Phase

Your investing strategy should shift depending on where the market is:

- **Recovery**: Buy undervalued assets, distressed properties, or value-add deals. Be bold but careful.

- **Expansion**: Grow strategically. Focus on cash flow and forced appreciation (renovations, repositioning).

- **Hyper Supply**: Be cautious. Sell underperforming assets, improve existing ones, and prepare for a downturn.

- **Recession**: Survive first. Look for great deals once prices drop. Keep strong reserves and avoid risky speculation.

And always no matter the phase stick to fundamentals. Don't buy just to buy. Make sure every property cash flows, every deal has a cushion, and your financing is solid.

Timing vs. Time in the Market

There's a popular saying in investing: "Time in the market beats timing the market." And in many ways, that's true. If you buy good properties, in good locations, and hold them for the long term, you'll likely do well even if you didn't catch the exact bottom or top of the cycle.

But being aware of timing gives you an edge. It helps you avoid buying in a frenzy or panicking during a dip. Long-term wealth in real estate isn't about flipping houses on a whim it's about accumulating cash-flowing assets and letting appreciation, debt pay down, and tax advantages do their work over time.

Still, smart timing based on data, not emotion, can make your journey faster and safer.

Final Thoughts: Be the Calm in the Cycle

Market cycles are natural. They're not something to fear they're something to understand. They create opportunities for those who are patient and prepared. The goal isn't to avoid risk entirely. It's to manage it, read the signals, and act when others hesitate.

The best investors aren't necessarily the smartest they're the most adaptable. They adjust their strategy when the cycle changes. They build during recovery, expand during growth, harvest during hyper supply, and stabilize during recession.

Your job as an investor isn't to predict the future it's to prepare for it. When you understand cycles, you stop reacting emotionally to headlines and start thinking like a long-term builder of wealth.

That's the mindset that wins in real estate. Not just once, but over and over again.

Risk Management and Due Diligence

The Hidden Side of Real Estate Wealth

Real estate, for all its promises of passive income and capital appreciation, is not without its shadows. Every profit opportunity carries a risk. And yet, most new investors focus almost exclusively on the upside: the cash flow projections, the appreciation potential, the ROI. Rarely do they ask, "What could go wrong?" In this chapter, we explore how professional investors manage risks, avoid disasters, and build resilience into their portfolios not by avoiding risk, but by confronting it with strategy and clarity.

Identifying the Risks

Before you can manage risk, you have to identify it. Real estate carries multiple categories of risk:

- **Market risk**: Where the local or national economy affects property values and rental income.

- **Tenant risk**: Such as late payments, property damage, or even lawsuits.

- **Liquidity risk**: Where selling a property quickly becomes difficult.

- **Legal and compliance risk**: Especially in regulated sectors like multi-family or short-term rentals.

- **Physical risk**: From structural issues to fire and natural disasters.

We explore how each of these risks manifests in real life through investor anecdotes and case studies. For example, a promising multifamily property in a growing city turned into a legal nightmare due to local zoning violations the investor never checked. Another investor bought a short-term rental property only to discover the city passed an ordinance banning Airbnb just months later. These stories are not outliers they are warnings and lessons.

The Due Diligence Process: Investigating Before You Invest

Due diligence is the investigative phase of real estate investing your opportunity to verify the deal is what it appears to be. Skipping or rushing this step is the fastest way to make expensive mistakes.

We divide the due diligence process into four core areas:

1. Property Inspection and Condition Assessment

This means hiring professionals to assess not just cosmetic appearance, but the foundation, roofing, electrical, HVAC, plumbing, pest control, mold, and more. A $10,000 inspection could save you $100,000 in deferred maintenance surprises.

One of the most common pitfalls is waiving inspections or removing contingencies too quickly just to win a deal. Sellers or agents in competitive markets may push for it, but doing so leaves you blind to hidden problems or financial risks. Contingencies are there to protect you use them wisely, and never sacrifice due diligence for speed.

2. Financial and Operational Review

You'll need to review existing leases, rent rolls, operating expenses, utility bills, taxes, and capital expenditures. If it's a rental property, compare actual income against pro forma projections. Never rely solely on the seller's numbers.

3. Legal and Title Due Diligence

Is the title clean? Are there liens, judgments, easements, or zoning changes on the horizon? You'll need a good real estate attorney to handle these checks, particularly on complex or commercial properties.

4. Neighborhood and Market Research

The property may be sound, but what about the neighborhood? Study local economic indicators, employment drivers, school quality, development plans, and crime rates. Many investors buy the right property in the wrong place.

Structuring for Protection: Legal and Financial Safeguards

Even with diligent research, risk remains. That's where proper structuring comes in. This section breaks down the key methods to insulate your personal and business finances:

- **Legal Entities**: Why you should never hold rental property in your personal name, and how LLCs, LPs, and trusts provide asset protection and tax advantages.

- **Insurance Layers**: From landlord policies and umbrella insurance to business interruption coverage, we explain what coverage you need and what is often overlooked.

- **Financing Risk**: Understanding loan terms, balloon payments, prepayment penalties, and how to structure financing conservatively even in bullish markets.

Contingency Planning: Expecting the Unexpected

A truly seasoned investor plans for the worst-case scenario not because they expect it, but because they know it's always possible. This final section explores:

- Creating reserve funds (Capex and operational)

- Stress-testing rental properties for 10–20% vacancy

- Planning exit strategies before buying: hold, refinance, flip, or wholesale

- Building relationships with professionals before emergencies hit

Common Pitfalls to Avoid

Even experienced investors can slip into avoidable mistakes. Here are some of the most common traps to watch for:

- Waiving inspections or removing contingencies too soon just to make an offer more attractive this can expose you to costly surprises.

- Relying only on appreciation to justify a deal instead of focusing on current cash flow.

- Failing to keep adequate reserves, leaving you unprepared for vacancies, repairs, or economic downturns.

- Overleveraging with too much debt relative to income, creating unnecessary stress and risk.

Conclusion: The Confident, Cautious Investor

Risk management and due diligence aren't about paranoia. They're about confidence through preparation. The goal isn't to eliminate risk (which is impossible), but to identify it, plan for it, and make educated decisions despite it. That's what separates professionals from amateurs.

Partnering for Profits: Joint Ventures and Syndications

Introduction: Scaling Beyond Solo Investing

At some point in every real estate investor's journey, they hit a wall. The wall may be time, capital, experience, or simply a lack of bandwidth. That's when the idea of partnering comes into play. When structured correctly, partnerships multiply strength and divide weakness. But when done poorly, they multiply problems and divide profits.

This chapter offers a deep dive into joint ventures and syndications two powerful vehicles to grow your portfolio by working with others. We explore how to structure them, protect yourself, and align everyone's interests.

Joint Ventures: Hands-On Partnerships with Shared Responsibility

Joint ventures are typically small-to-medium-sized partnerships where two or more investors actively participate in a deal. For example, one person brings the capital, another handles the renovations, and both share decision-making and profits.

We break down:

- **Legal structure and documentation**: How to draft clear operating agreements with equity splits, voting rights, and dispute resolution.

- **Choosing the right partner**: It's not just about complementary skills shared values and vision are more important.

- **Risk and reward balancing**: How to allocate profits fairly while managing responsibilities, timelines, and liabilities.

You'll also find common pitfalls to avoid, such as over-promising, lack of communication, or failure to document verbal agreements.

Syndications: Pooling Capital for Larger Deals

Syndications involve raising money from multiple passive investors to fund a real estate deal usually larger commercial or multifamily projects. In a syndication, there are two key roles:

- **The sponsor or general partner (GP)**: Finds, underwrites, and manages the deal.

- **The limited partners (LPs)**: Contribute capital but have no day-to-day responsibilities.

This section explores:

- **SEC compliance**: Understanding exemptions, accredited investor rules, and private placement memorandums (PPMs).

- **Waterfall structures**: Preferred returns, equity splits, and performance bonuses for GPs.

- **Investor relations**: Communicating transparently and managing expectations.

You'll also learn how to raise capital legally and ethically, including the difference between 506(b) and 506(c) offerings, and why trust and reputation are your greatest assets in syndication.

Partnerships that Last: Communication, Alignment, and Exit Plans

Many partnerships break down not because of bad deals, but because of poor communication and unclear expectations. This section focuses on:

- Establishing regular reporting and financial transparency

- Aligning short-term and long-term goals

- Handling conflict, mediation, and partner exits

Every partnership should be structured with an exit strategy in mind. What happens if someone wants to sell early? Becomes ill? Passes away? Plans for these "what ifs" must be built into the legal framework upfront.

Conclusion: Leveraging People for Bigger Opportunities

Partnerships, when formed intentionally, are rocket fuel. They allow you to do bigger deals, access better financing, and grow faster than you ever could alone. But they require maturity, trust, and structure. Done right, they're not just profitable they're transformative.

Creative and Alternative Strategies

When the Market Says "No," You Say "How?"

Sometimes, the conventional path is blocked. Prices are too high, lenders are too strict, and inventory is scarce. That's when successful investors reach into their toolbox and pull out creative strategies. This chapter is about learning to invest with flexibility, innovation, and resourcefulness skills that separate deal-makers from deal-seekers.

Seller Financing: Buying Without Banks

When banks say "no," the seller might say "yes." Seller financing involves the seller acting as the lender, allowing the buyer to make payments over time.

We cover:

- **Structuring win-win terms**: down payments, interest rates, balloon payments

- **Legal protections and promissory notes**

- **Pros** (flexibility, speed) and **cons** (seller risk, due diligence)

- **Example**: A real-world deal where a seller-financed duplex enabled a first-time investor to bypass bank hurdles

Lease Options and Rent-to-Own Models

With a lease option, you rent the property now with the option to buy later at an agreed-upon price. This can be a low-cost way to control property with upside potential.

We discuss:

- Option fees, strike prices, and lease terms

- Why this is great for investors and useful for homeowners who want flexibility

- Legal precautions to avoid being classified as a sale (in case of default)

Wholesaling: Profit Without Property Ownership

Wholesaling is a strategy where you find off-market deals, get them under contract, and assign the contract to another investor for a fee. It requires hustle, negotiation, and marketing but little to no capital.

We explore:

- **Lead generation strategies**: Driving for dollars, direct mail, cold calling

- **Contract structure and assignment clauses**

- **Local laws and ethical considerations**

- **Transitioning from wholesaling to ownership**

The BRRRR Method, House Hacking, and Airbnb Arbitrage

In this section, we explore hybrid, high-impact strategies:

- **BRRRR** (Buy, Rehab, Rent, Refinance, Repeat): How to recycle capital and scale a rental portfolio.

- **House hacking**: Living in a duplex or renting rooms to eliminate housing costs.

- **Airbnb arbitrage**: Renting properties long-term, then re-renting them as short-term stays (with landlord permission).

These approaches are great for low-capital investors looking to accelerate returns.

Alternative Asset Classes: Storage, Land, Mobile Homes, and More

To end the chapter, we go deeper into niche markets:

- **Mobile home parks**: High cash flow, low turnover, but complex regulation.

- **Self-storage**: Recession-resistant, low maintenance.

- **Raw land**: Cheap to buy, but speculative and slow to produce income.

- **Tiny homes, co-living, and modular housing**: The future of affordable housing?

These alternatives offer new frontiers for creative investors ready to think outside the box.

Conclusion: Creativity is the Investor's Greatest Tool

Creative strategies aren't "Plan B" they're often the unseen Plan A that others miss. In tight markets or uncertain times, creativity unlocks deals, generates cash flow, and keeps you moving forward. Mastering these tools means you'll never be at the mercy of the market again.

Your Next Move: Putting It All Into Action

By now, you've traveled the full arc of the real estate investing journey from mindset and market selection to financing, management, and scaling. The final chapter of this book is not about adding more information; it's about turning knowledge into action. Without implementation, even the most powerful real estate strategy remains an idea. Whether you're just beginning or ready to expand, your success lies in what you do next. This chapter provides a practical blueprint for building momentum and moving forward with purpose.

Revisiting Your Investment Vision

Before moving forward, take a moment to reconnect with your "why." Are you pursuing financial independence, time freedom, or a family legacy? Clarity of purpose will guide your decision-making and keep you focused when challenges arise. With a defined goal in mind, revisit the strategies and concepts that align most with your vision. Not every approach is right for every investor; your journey should reflect your values, lifestyle preferences, and long-term aspirations.

Assessing Where You Are Today

Every investor starts from a unique place. You may be a complete beginner with limited capital, or an experienced investor looking to optimize an existing portfolio. Assess your current financial position, your knowledge base, your available time, and your personal risk tolerance. Identify your greatest strengths whether it's capital, access to deals, or project management and also acknowledge your current limitations. This self-awareness will help you craft a more realistic and effective action plan.

Designing Your Personal Investment Roadmap

Your roadmap should include both short-term objectives and long-term vision. A strong plan might span the next 12 months, with milestones each quarter for education, networking, analysis, and acquisition. Set specific targets, such as evaluating 50 deals, speaking to 10 lenders, or purchasing your first duplex. Long-term, define what success looks like in 3 years and 10 years. Your roadmap is a living document, and it should evolve as your knowledge, experience, and financial situation grow.

Taking Action in the Next 90 Days

The most critical time for an investor is the beginning. The first 90 days of focused effort can set the stage for years of success. Start by choosing a market to research thoroughly, building a small team of professionals, and identifying financing options that fit your goals. Analyze real deals, attend local investor meetups, and make offers even if they don't get accepted right away. Action beats perfection. Each step forward, no matter how small, builds momentum and confidence.

Staying Accountable and Committed

Consistency beats intensity in real estate. Set up accountability systems whether through mentors, masterminds, or tracking tools to ensure you follow through on your goals. Real estate investing comes with inevitable ups and downs, but commitment to the process is what separates successful investors from spectators. Celebrate small wins, review progress regularly, and recalibrate your strategy as needed. The journey is long, but deeply rewarding for those who stay the course.

Committing to Lifelong Learning

The real estate landscape is always evolving. Market trends shift, laws change, and new tools emerge. Make a habit of continuous education. Read books, listen to podcasts, take advanced courses, and surround yourself with experienced investors. Growth doesn't stop once you own property; in fact, that's when the most important learning begins. Being a student of the game ensures you remain adaptive and competitive for years to come.

Final Words: You Are Ready

You now possess the blueprint, the tools, and the perspective to take control of your financial future through real estate. The time to start or to take your next leap is now. There will never be a perfect moment, but there will always be an opportunity for those who act with courage and intention. Remember, every great investor once stood where you stand now full of questions, but willing to begin. Let this book be your foundation, and let your actions write the next chapter of your real estate journey.

Review statements / Acknowledgments

"David S Phung brings a wealth of local market knowledge and professionalism to the real estate industry. As a licensed agent based in Sacramento, California, he offers his clients exclusive access to real-time market data and expert guidance.

David is dedicated to helping buyers and sellers navigate the complexities of the market with confidence. His commitment to transparency, data-driven insights, and personalized service makes him a trusted advisor for anyone looking to make informed real estate decisions.

This book is a testament to his expertise and serves as a valuable resource for anyone looking to succeed in real estate."

Brent Gove

Team Leader / Realtor

"From Start to Finish, David has given you all the information you need to step into your Real Estate Dreams!"

Barry Mathis

Broker, Property Manager, Investor
Certified Investment Expert
CDPE/ CIPE/ AARE/ NCREA

"Putting your Real Estate to work for you via house hacking, renting monthly, or doing short-term rentals is a great way to become wealthy."

TJ Roberts

Sales Team Lead, Branch Manager, NMLS ID# 1457455
Paramount Residential Mortgage Group, Inc.

"David, you do a great job showing people that you care and that you know your stuff when it comes to real estate in Sacramento. You sound kind, smart, and easy to trust, which is super important when someone is buying or selling a home.

What's great:

Your Story: You talk about growing up in Sacramento and why you got into real estate. That helps people feel connected to you.

Helping People: You focus on what your clients need. You let them know you're here to make things easier and less stressful. That's something everyone wants!

Friendly Ending: You invite people to reach out and talk to you. It feels welcoming, not pushy.

Ideas to make it even better:

What Makes You Special? Maybe tell people one or two things that make you different from other agents. Do you know a lot about a certain neighborhood? Or maybe you're really good at helping first-time buyers?

Overall, you come across as honest and helpful."

Scott Vogeli

Modern Edison Electric

I've known David for many years, and during that time, I've come to deeply respect not just his real estate expertise, but his character, integrity, and dedication to serving others. I've hosted numerous open houses for David, referred him to some of my most valued clients, and even reached out to him for guidance on topics beyond real estate, including insurance and local resources. His generosity with knowledge and time has always stood out.

David's latest book, *The Ultimate Real Estate Guide*, is a powerful reflection of the way he approaches his work: with clarity, patience, and incredible attention to detail. What I appreciate most is how accessible and thorough he is whether he's breaking down the 1031 Exchange or explaining the role of escrow. This isn't just another real estate book. It's a practical, well-organized manual built on real experience, written in a voice that feels like you're sitting down with a mentor who wants to see you succeed.

As a fellow author and someone deeply committed to empowering my community especially Spanish-speaking families through financial literacy I see in David's writing that same purpose: to educate, uplift, and guide. His community focus and heart for service are part of what have always helped us connect so easily.

David isn't just a real estate expert he's a true professional who cares, and this book is proof of that.

Boris E. Vasquez

Real Estate & Mortgage Broker, Tax Consultant
NMLS # 1520547

I enjoyed reading the book. What I liked best was that it was concise, clear, and easy to read and understand.

The book provided a good foundation of the real estate process in purchasing a home. It also added additional valuable information to parties other than being a first-time homebuyer.

Thank you for sharing the information with me.

Wishing you much success with the book.

Lay Xaochay

Chicago Title Company

Branch Manager/Escrow Officer

Elk Grove, CA 95758

License Number 2993-4

Great job!

And good luck. 😊

Joel Wright

Real Estate Market
Strategist & Data Enthusiast
Residential Round Up 2025 Speaker

It seems straightforward!

Good luck to you.

Chanh Nguyen

EXp Realty of California, Inc.
Lic: 01727144

Thanks for sharing the book. I went through it over the weekend and spent a few hours reading it. I really enjoyed it. Your passion for helping others find their purpose is clear throughout.

The mix of personal stories, research, and real-life examples made it engaging. I especially liked the Flow Journal and Compliment Tracker exercises.

Chapter 9 was a highlight connecting personal growth with real careers like insurance and real estate was smart and practical.

Great work overall I'm sure it'll inspire a lot of readers.

Sam Aoude

CEO, Wealth Land Corp.
Laguna Hills, CA 92653 United States of America

"We do wish you the best in your endeavors."

Carrisi Huffman

Student Support
The Michael Blank Brands – Support

"That is so cool. Congratulations."

Ryan Lundquist

Certified Residential Appraiser
Private appraisals & consulting

We're always glad to hear about the great work our members are doing.

Spencer High

Manager, Media | Communications
NATIONAL ASSOCIATION OF REALTORS® | 500 New Jersey Ave NW | Washington, DC 20001

"Good luck."

KIRSTIN CORMAN

Vice President, Concierge REALTOR®
Legacy Properties Sotheby's International Realty
46 Bay View Street, Camden, Maine 04843

"That's great. Good luck with the book."

Warm regards,

Avery Bibbs

Accountant Executive
Northern California
Leader 1031
National Headquarters
180 Massachusetts Ave.
Arlington, MA, 02474

"As I read *Investing and Growing Wealth through Real Estate* by David S Phung, I found myself captivated by its practical, mentorship-driven approach, which empowered me to see real estate as a powerful tool for building wealth, whether I'm just starting out or looking to refine my investment strategy. Drawing from his Sacramento-based experience as a realtor and entrepreneur, Phung delivers a comprehensive guide that's both accessible and detailed, covering market cycles, financing options like the BRRRR method, tax strategies such as 1031 exchanges, and creative approaches like wholesaling and seller financing. His relatable anecdotes, actionable 90-day plan, and emphasis on treating investing like a business inspired me to approach real estate with discipline and confidence, making this book an invaluable resource for achieving financial independence."

Erich Scharf

SACINSPECT, INC
2701 Del Paso Suite 130-502
Sacramento, CA. 95835

Great book!

"This book offers a thorough and insightful guide to leveraging real estate as a powerful tool for building wealth. It clearly outlines various strategies and approaches, making complex concepts accessible and actionable. I strongly believe that this curriculum should be integrated into high school education, as it equips young people with essential financial literacy and practical knowledge that can shape their futures."

Precious McClain

Over a decade in Property Management
California Real Estate Lic
CCRM (California Certified Property Manager)

"As a fellow professional in real estate, I truly enjoyed reading your book. My favorite part was Chapter 12, where you discuss implementation and specifically what we would like our investor audience to achieve within the next 90 days. It is very well-written, straightforward, and, most importantly, extremely implementable. Well done!

Anyone who reads this book will benefit. I even learned a few new things, and I've been in the industry for over 30 years. Knowledge is power."

Ben Soifer

Founder and Creator of the CIDC Course for Commercial Investment Debt Consultants who are looking to be Financial Freedom Ambassadors

Ben Soifer | Soifer Group

CIDC, Commercial Investment Debt Consultant

www.moneymanagement.today

As a licensed California real estate broker since 2010 and specializing in private money financing for over 20 years, I found David S Phung's Investing and Growing Wealth Through Real Estate to be an excellent resource for both new and seasoned investors. David blends practical strategies with real-world insights in a way that is clear, actionable, and grounded in integrity. His focus on fundamentals financing, risk management, and creative deal structures makes this book a valuable guide for anyone serious about building long-term wealth through real estate. I highly recommend it.

Craig Cox,

California Real Estate Broker Lic 01884300

"Buying a homes is one of the most challenging obstacles our country faces to achieve financial freedom, But the Ultimate Real Estate Guide, by David S. Phung, has made it a little easier. This book entails details from start to finish. As a mortgage professional, the key points such as what to expect, how to save, and even gets down to the technicalities of assets, credit and income, I was amazed. Similar books guide your through the process without giving you specifics details on what to expect during the approval phase. Some of the biggest challenges I see borrowers face everyday is income and assets, but Mr. Phung hit it on the nail with providing realistic expectations we face in the market today. I highly recommend reading if you are planning to buy or sell your home. This book is easy to read and keeps the reader engaged while also teaching the ins and outs of our real estate market today".

Codi Cross,

Mortgage professional

"I do think it's impressive that you wrote this book and look forward to you hopefully having successful sales of it".

Ethan Conrad

CEO
Ethan Conrad Properties Inc.
DRE: 01298662

"Great job David in putting this book on real estate investing together. Best wishes!".

Jerry Rivera

Compass
REALTOR® | DRE#01376115
Licensed as: Gerardo Rivera
Masters Club - Outstanding Life Member
Sacramento, CA 9581

Real Estate Resources

A curated list of trusted resources to support buyers, sellers, and investors throughout their real estate journey:

Real Estate Investment Trusts (REITs)

www.investor.gov

National Association of Realtors

www.realtor.com

www.nar.realtor

National Real Estate Investors Association

www.nationalreia.org

CCIM Institute

www.ccim.com

REITs and Real Estate Investing

www.reit.com

CFA Institute

www.cfainstitute.org

Bankrate – Independent, advertising-supported publisher and comparison service

www.bankrate.com

NAIOP – The Commercial Real Estate Development Association

www.naiop.org

National Association of Residential Property Managers (NARPM)

www.sacramento.narpm.org

www.narpm.org

The California Apartment Association

www.caanet.org

Property Management Association

www.pma-dc.org

BOMA/BOMI – The Commercial Real Estate Trade Association

www.boma.org

Vacation Rental Management Association

www.vrma.org

Institute of Real Estate Management (IREM)

www.irem.org

Building Owners and Managers Association of California (BOMA California)

www.cbpa.com

www.boma-california

California NARPM

www.narpmcalifornia.org

Community Associations Institute (CAI)

www.caionline.org

National Affordable Housing Management Association

www.nahma.org

IFMA – International Facility Management Association

www.ifma.org